Information Security based on VDA ISA TISAX Automotive Strategies

A Leadership Introduction to Information Security in the Automotive Industry

Christian Bartsch

1st English Edition 2023

ACATO BOOKS

ACATO BOOKS

USA | UK | EU | Canada | Australia
India | Mexico | Brazil |Japan

ACATO Books is part of ACATO GmbH
whose addresses can be found at acato.de

First published in USA by ACATO Books in 2023
First published in UK by ACATO Books in 2023
First published in ACATO Books in 2023

ISBN: 979-8-8650-6265-3 Softcover

ASIN: B0CNPQS83W Kindle Edition

Publisher's DISCLAIMER

Any internet address, phone numbers, or company or product information printed in this book are offered as a resource and are not intended in any way to be or to imply an endorsement by ACATO Books, nor does ACATO Books vouch for the existence, content, or services of these sites, phone numbers, companies, or products beyond the life of this book. All reasonable efforts have been made to correctly attribute the intellectual property of unique concepts of others. Every person referenced in this book has been contacted by the author to have their quotes, concepts or information approved.

Revision-No. 1.01 ENG / 2023-12-28 — 13-11

CONTENTS

1 Introduction

The automotive industry has been one of the key motors of quality management initiatives. Eventually other industries adopted similar approach to **quality control and improvement**. This is why it is so important for medium to large businesses to have an ISO 9001 certification. As the world of **automotive manufacturing** becomes an even more digital business, it is necessary to protect the intellectual property stored in information big automotive brands share with their suppliers. This also expands to components that are highly integrated in a digital way. Hence, TISAX eventually became the key cyber security standard. If you are new to TISAX then you might be aware of **ISO 27001 Standard**, that is related to information security. The **2022 Release** of the ISO 27001 Standard is now emphasizing the importance of **data privacy and cyber security**.

At this point your mind should start asking these questions:

- Why should my company achieve a high TISAX level?
- When does my company need to start a TISAX project?
- How can we generate a sustainable outcome?

Let's face it. It can be quite frustrating to see revenue fall, just because your company did not invest the effort into getting ISO 27001 certified or even reaching any **assessment level of TISAX**. Let me now show you in an informative and hopefully also useful way how you **get ready for a TISAX assessment**. If you follow this rapid introduction to cyber security in the automotive industry, you will experience a better outcome for your company's future.

From personal experience in the automotive industry, I understand how complex and challenging is doing business for suppliers with large car manufacturers.

Today I am no longer working in the automotive industry, since I have transitioned into the world of **information security** and <u>standard related auditing</u> (ISO 9001, ISO 27001).

Today, I advise companies on, <u>how to get their ISMS documentation ready for certification</u>. My clients are SMEs, European holdings and technology driven manufacturers. As I am also active on the auditing side, I understand what large certification bodies expect to be a compliant **Information Security Management System** (ISMS). TISAX and ISO 27001 can put substantial pressure on an organisation, if the project becomes bloated. I want you to avoid running into useless courses, overpriced advice and outdated templates that force you to act against your gut feeling.

Yours

Christian Bartsch

PS: If you would like to get advice on how to …, don't hesitate to contact me at c.bartsch@acato.de.

Do you need more strategical insights before the day?

Get the strategy book: books.meetchrisbartsch.com

Trust me: it is worthwhile the effort to mind feed now!

2 Why TISAX matters in the Automotive Industry?

In the following sections I will answer for you following questions:

- Why should I care as an executive?
- How can TISAX be explained to me in short and simple terms?
- Hat impact will it have on my success?
- Where will I feel pain if I ignore TISAX?
- What can be done?

As you notice, above questions gradually guide you into understanding the impact of TISAX and how to best tackle TISAX so you do not have to suffer any negative impact. If you do experience unforeseen stress due to TISAX this might be an indicator that you are not taking advantage of its positive opportunities.

2.1 What is TISAX?

Let me introduce you to TISAX in a compact and understandable language: The German association of the automotive industry (**VDA**) introduced the TISAX as a benchmark for evaluation of information security and data protection capabilities.

The abbreviation "TISAX" stands for **Trusted Information Security Assessment Exchange**.

TISAX is used by the automotive industry to reach a standard or assessing the security level of information technology systems of companies, which might become suppliers or joint venture partners.

Hence, TISAX is a **cyber security assessment framework**. By agreeing on TISAX as a common assessment and evaluation framework, the German automotive industry has **simplified the process of benchmarking suppliers**. Thereby, suppliers have less workload in demonstrating their cyber security commitment.

Before TISAX every major automotive manufacturer had very different benchmark systems in place. This strained suppliers who needed very different documentation to satisfy the regulations of each key client.

With introduction of TISAX suppliers could focus more on one common standard, which had been designed on the learnings of the **ISO 27001 Standard**.

As automation is increasingly becoming a digital inter-connected part of an automotive company's competitive advantage, **cyber-attacks are a significant operational risk**. Hackers are known to have gained access to the networks of a German automaker for over 6 months. During that time, hackers were able to access confidential design, research and operative data.

The digital **theft of trade secrets** is a substantial threat to the western automotive industry. TISAX tries to address these substantial threats.

Companies that are compliant with the requirements of TISAX can **build trust with their customers, partners and suppliers**. Governments are increasingly aware of the cyber risks looming in the automotive sector as vehicles are increasingly turning into autonomous vehicles.

Hackers, cyber terrorists and digital warfare can **disrupt society and the economy** of a nation.

2.2   TISAX can become a competitive advantages

TISAX is used by organizations to **improve their cyber resilience and manage cyber threats** in a more sustainable way. Thereby, organizations become aware of the current cyber risks and the potential existential harm a breach could cause. Not only manufacturing can be disrupted, but also unforeseen product risks could evolve from attackers intentional manipulation of the manufacturing process.

This commitment to TISAX allows companies to **display their full commitment** to ensuring an acceptable level of cyber security to protect all stakeholders. Hence, a company with TISAX implementation will be perceived as a trusted business partner.

Large automotive manufacturers implement a just-in-time and lean management strategy. A security breach at a supplier can disrupt the entire supply chain and costs millions per day, as production comes to a painful stand still. A company using TISAX will not be able to prevent every security breach, but it will have done everything one should expect of them to prevent it from causing harm to others.

Hence, TISAX sets **best practices** for managing information security, **facilitating collaboration** and **building trust** between companies of all sorts (e.g., Suppliers, Manufacturers, Designers, Research Institutes).

Being compliant with TISAX increases a company's attractiveness as a business partner. By being able to **demonstrate the high level of information security**, they will grow their business opportunities. Large manufacturers will be more willing to favour their offerings over that of non-compliant suppliers. This compliance turns into a competitive advantage when entering new markets and long term supply arrangements.

Large automotive manufacturers are constantly looking for suppliers in all fields and countries, as technology is rapidly advancing. Only relying on one suppliers for a particular part can become the tripping stone for a major automotive brand. Similar examples exist in the crisis surrounding *airbag and brake manufacturers* of foreign automotive manufacturers. Such crisis can lead to low level of trust in the eye of <u>authorities and customers</u>.

The automotive industry is used to having to comply with many regulations imposed by many countries, which cause additional costs just because of some requirement based on an outdated ideology in the minds of the political establishment (e.g. yellow headlights).

By using TISAX efficiently they can also become **better equipped to meet regulatory requirements**. In the USA every different state has differing laws in regards to sales, information security and taxation which affect manufacturers and their dealership networks. In Europe similar national peculiarities can cause additional complexity headaches even though the European Union has implemented standard regulations such as GDPR.

The investment in TISAX helps them prove to the relevant authorities, that they are taking the necessary steps to **protect sensible data**. Therefore, they are <u>complying with laws and regulations</u>.

Let me summarize what TISAX does for you:

- Helps manage risks and improve security
- Establishes companies as trusted partners
- Compliance increases competitive advantages
- Meet legal and regulatory requirements

Large manufacturers benefit from TISAX as it allows them to build a reliable and trusted supply chain.

3 The true nature of TISAX

TISAX is designed as a scalable and flexible framework adaptable to all types of organizations. This allows **small suppliers and large OEMs** to implement TISAX in a fashion that matches their individual characteristics.

In contrast to other standards, a company does not receive a certificate after audit, but the audit provider (also known as certification body) **submits its report** to the ENX association. Once this have been approved by ENX, the report statement is published only on the enx.com website.

When participating in TISAX one has to choose to be **providing or assessing assessment information or both**. An audit firm (e.g. TÜV Süd) would be acting as the assessing assessment information. In contrast, a brakes manufacturer would be a providing assessment information. Some large car manufacturers often assess their suppliers with their own audit teams. In that case they are acting in both roles, since at some point they will be assessed, too.

ENX is the body **maintaining the audit provider criteria** and **assessment requirements** (TISAX ACAR). It approves audit providers. ENX monitors the quality of implementation as well as the assessment results. ENX is supported by the TISAX Committee. The TISAX Committee consists of representatives from manufacturers, suppliers and associations.

In order for ENX to be able to enforce transparent governance, ENX has set rules that help prevent fake certificates being used in any business transaction where TISAX is a criteria. The control function is protected by a **contract structure** in which ENX holds contracts with all **stakeholders**, including the audit providers and the participants. This ensures that the results correspond to the desired objectivity and quality. The **rights and duties** of all participants – small or large – are respected.

3.1 History of TISAX

As previously mentioned, TISAX was introduced by the German automotive industry association. Its objective was to create a common ground for *cyber security assessments*, which goes beyond ISO 27001.After years of <u>continued improvement</u>, TISAX is accepted as a leading framework for information security management.

3.2 Who conducts TISAX assessments?

Only accredited certification bodies (*a.k.a. assessors*) may conduct assessments upon which a type of certificate is issues. This assessment conclusion document highlights the level of cyber security found in that organization.

Following organisations are examples of accredited audit providers:

- TÜV Süd

- TÜV Nord

- DEKRA

- KPMG

You can find a regional list of audit providers on this website:

https://enx.com/en-US/TISAX/xap/

Hence, organizations will receive recognition for their outstanding initiatives to ensure a level of information security.

3.3 TISAX Standard Requirements

According to the TISAX Standard, organizations are expected to implement a comprehensive information security management system (ISMS). The ISMS needs to contain all aspects of <u>cyber security, risk management, incident management</u>, and <u>access control</u>.

In regards to risk management, organizations should maintain a risk management process that ensures regular evaluation of its cyber security, as well as identification and management of risks in a rapidly changing world. By implementing a process for incident management, organizations are able to respond to threats in a more resilient way. They gain the ability to detect and respond to incidents. Business continuity is highly dependent on their ability to restore operations after an incident.

Furthermore, the protection of **prototype related data** is a key requirement of TISAX. New vehicles undergo a development period of 3 to 5 years. Hereby, many suppliers share data with other suppliers and their key client. Theft and manipulation of prototype data can have severe impact for production and product safety. That is why manufacturers make a great effort to **protect valuable** and confidential information. Protecting prototypes expands beyond the digital world by including **physical and logical access controls.** Here, data encryption adds an additional layer of protection.

TISAX expects organizations to enforce a level of data protection, which requires them to **implement security controls** to protect personal data (e.g., customer data, employee data) from **unauthorized access, manipulation and misuse**. The implementation of technical and organizational measures are similar to that of ISO 27001. These measures are designed to ensure **confidentiality, integrity and availability** of the data. This expands towards meeting the requirements of data protection laws (e.g., BDSG) and related regulations (e.g., GDPR).

Hence, the key items are:
- risk management
- Incident management
- Prototype protection
- Protection of data privacy

In order to be TISAX certified, an organization must implement the standard's requirements. Auditors will inspect the ISMS documentation and a variety of records, in order to evaluate the true level of compliance of an organization.

3.4 The TISAX Assessment process

During the TISAX assessment auditors will follow a comprehensive and systematic approach. Like with ISO 27001, TISAX auditors will follow a structured process whereby they evaluate, if **the documentation reflects true adoption** of the standard or represents a fake compliance. Most professional organizations will have the financial and organizational resources to take TISAX seriously.

The benefit of such an assessment is a range of key learnings, which will **help improve an organization's nature**. Hence, preparing for the assessment must consist of management commitment and gaining support from the entire workforce. This support will need to go beyond company borders as some suppliers may have a critical influence in the success of an ongoing TISAX Compliance.

These key items need to be achieved before the preparation phase is completed:

- Understand the standard's requirements
- Understand the scope of the audit
- Plan the ISMS implementation

These key items need to be achieved before the **implementation phase** is completed:

- Write all relevant ISMS documents
- Develop policies, procedures and processes
- Gather all relevant operational information
- Evaluate potential weaknesses and resolve them
- Train staff (incl. awareness trainings)
- Communicate to staff the next phase

These steps take place during the **assessment phase**:

- Request assessment from certification body
- Evaluation of key documentation (ISMS)

- Review of policies, procedures and processes
- On-site assessments to gather evidence of effective implementation
- Resolution of identified deficiencies
- Adapting security measures to resolve issues
- Prove of corrective resolution of weaknesses
- Implementation of recommended improvements

These steps take place during the **certification phase**:

- The auditor provides a report and relevant evidence of the assessed level of compliance to the certification body.
- The certification body reviews the submitted documents and the auditor's recommendation for certification
- The certification body approves certification and issues the TISAX certificate

3.5 Types of TISAX Assessment

Organisations have a choice of 2 types of assessments. Each is type is designed to the specific needs and requirements of different types of organizations.

TISAX offers these types of assessment:
- TISAX Basic Assessment
- TISAX Advanced Assessment

TISAX Basic Assessment

Organizations just starting to implement an Information Security Management system (ISMS) are well advised to start with the TISAX Basic Assessment. This assessment focuses the core requirements of the TISAX Standard.

This will also require inspection of:
- implementation of a security policy,
- risk management process,
- incident management process and
- the access controls

After this assessment one will receive a report identifying **all areas of non-compliance**. This document will also state <u>recommendations for improvement</u>.

Only after resolving all identified issues and making use of the recommendations, one should consider embarking on the next route towards a TISAX Advanced Assessment.

TISAX Advanced Assessment

The second type of assessment is called "**TISAX Advanced Assessment**" and is <u>only suitable for organizations with an existing and well established ISMS</u>. The benefit of working towards this higher level of assessment is, that the security level of the organization will be further strengthened.

Since information security requires not only technical and organizational measures to **ensure proper implementation**, one needs to also consider the human impact on security. Humans need time to adapt to change and turn the new ways of work into a natural habit. After the first introduction of an ISMS organizations will typically experience some levels of resistance. Building <u>awareness</u> and gaining honest <u>commitment</u> to a new standard takes time.

The TISAX Advanced Assessment **sets higher expectations** as advanced requirements need to be met by the organization. This leads to an implementation of sophisticated security controls (e.g., continuous monitoring, vulnerability management, penetration testing, etc.).

After completing the TISAX Advanced Assessment, the organization will **receive a more detailed report**. Due to the intensity of the audit, more insights will be gained though the auditors feedback. The greater range of assessment will be a greater strain on the organization as they are expected to demonstrate a **higher level of compliance** with the TISAX Standard.

These so called baseline and extended assessments need to be conducted by independent auditors (a.k.a. assessors). They are trained and certified in the TISAX Standard.

These assessments are quite detailed and impartial in order to help organizations improve their security. Thereby, they will be better at protecting sensitive data and systems.

By applying the TISAX Framework, organizations gain access to its tools and guidance. This way, they can implement an effective ISMS.

3.6 Typical misunderstandings

One must be careful with the terms *"information security"* and *"cyber security"*, as they are often used in the wrong context. Cyber security is a **subsection of information security**. information security protects digital (*e.g. files*) and physical assets (*e.g., paper records*).

4 Getting ready for TISAX

In order to succeed with implementation and assessment, organizations need to prepare well. The documentation needs to match the requirements of TISAX. Too often templates purchased from the web are incomplete or even outdated. This is similar to what you can run into when hoping for a shortcut to ISO 27001 certification.

It is best practice to write a project plan and have a checklist at hand, so that one doesn't miss important items. Some organizations conduct an internal GAP analysis and then request an external advisor to run a second GAP analysis when all documentation is completed and every person in the organization is actually using the new way of working with sensitive information.

4.1 Gap Analysis

In order to know how far developed the organization is before implementation of a TISAX compliant ISMS, one should assess the current situation. This is where a GAP analysis provides a realistic picture of the **existing security** and what still needs to improve. This way, the project team can prioritize the key issues to work on.

By using the TISAX framework as a guide towards an information security management system (ISMS), the organization will be able to not only comply with TISAX but also adjust its ISMS to fit the organization's **unique business model**.

In many cases security will have been implemented as a technical feature in the IT Department. There might be some kind of documentation on how Active Directory, Firewalls, VPN and other IT Technology has been configured to match the current opinion on how to implement IT security. Unfortunately, information security is a large topic which includes many other items such as IT security or cyber security.

If there is some kind of documentation then this will help formulate the policies in the ISMs. Hence, a GAP Analysis will look at security policies, procedures and controls. These need to be compared to the requirements of TISAX. This eventually feeds into the to do list or checklist for building a compliant ISMS.

In order to ensure a realistic data collection, one will need to **speak to a variety of key people** (e.g., IT admins, CSO, IT Directors, Network Admins, Developers, Engineers, etc.) in the organization. Besides communication with technical staff, one needs to also communicate with **sales, marketing, logistics, facility management, procurement, HR** and other departments and locations.

Identifying **risks and vulnerabilities** helps establish a better understanding of the organizations current risk exposure. One can't expect in an organization that every employee knows what an ISMS is or how it relates to their individual work place. Hence, a first part of the communication during GAP analysis is to build awareness what information security actually means for the employee and the organization as a whole.

4.2 Compliance Roadmap

As part of every ISMS related project, an organization needs to first develop a project plan. This is an advisable step that doesn't need to consume a lot of work time but can **avoid costly gaps** in a growing project. Whether you are building an ISMS in accordance with TISAX or ISO 27001 you will realize, that this is often like walking through a jungle. You gradually detect issues you were not previously aware off. You might even notice that you overlooked a requirement, because there is so much to be done.

Most people who are writing an ISMS an employee - of a to be certified organization - are doing this for the first time in their life. This is also a learning opportunity this person.

Follow these 4 steps:

- Identify gaps
- Rank identified gaps
- Select order of urgency
- Fix the gaps

Focus your time and energy on the most critical areas. Get your ISMS to be compliant with TISAX within a reasonable time frame. If you keep leaving the project collecting dust for weeks, you will waste more resources having to reevaluate your progress and the gaps.

Next will be to **define the goals and activities** which need to be part of each step in your compliance road map. Look at your **security policies**: develop them and document them according to TISAX. Are your procedures well defined and written so that any reasonable person understands how to proceed?

Look at your technical controls: What do you have currently in place? Read the documentation created by your technical staff. Write your own <u>clean and standardized document</u> for each technical control. In order to not forget any vital items, use sharable sheets (e.g. google sheets or SharePoint). **Mind maps** also help to drill down in order to find forgotten items. Check with your technical staff to find out any <u>new or outdated item being left out</u> on the list.

A with every roadmap, you should **set mile stones**. By assigning dates to each waypoint you will be able to **track bottlenecks and efficiency**. Management will most likely want a simple *bi-weekly report on your current progress*. Keep it simple by using a visible flow diagram, which you can <u>update within a **few** minutes</u>.

You can also **list the required resources** (e.g., budget, people, tools, documents) and departments (e.g., Network Admins, Accounting, HR Trainers) below every step. Be careful <u>not to overload</u> your visual roadmap. As your project progresses, you will find the need to **add outside expertise** (e.g., consulting) and **technology** (e.g., DMZ, VPN, new phones). Without the adequate budget you will be misled to seek the cheapest outside resource, that will only help you for a limited amount of time or threats.

Once you have a clear picture of what needs to be done in which order and have **considered any critical dependencies**, then you can reach out to a greater amount of people to get feedback on the new compliance road map.

As with every business, there are times in the year when migrating critical systems, upgrading manufacturing facilities or introducing a new ISMS can cause severe problems in the operational flow of the business.

Hence, check not only with stakeholders about the goals you set and the roadmap but also **gain their advice on dates**, that can cause severe operational disruption. This way you <u>reduce the stress on the organization</u> during your introduction of the new ISMS into the productive side of the business. Collect the feedback and evaluate their concerns or challenges. Adapt your time plan to avoid bottlenecks and distress.

4.2.1 TISAX implementation team

The TISAX implementation team should consist of following team members

- Security expert (knows the TISAX Standard)
- Business expert (knows business processes and requirements)
- Representatives from key departments (e.g., sales, legal, HR)

These people will be needed to **assist in the implementation** of the processes. Thereby you will gain approval and activate the necessary processes **with less resistance**. Eventually you will achieve that business goals align with the ISMS. By assigning clear roles and responsibilities to each team member, you avoid conflicts and unnecessary duplication of tasks. That is how to complete the project in time and without excessive budget overstrain.

As you prepare to roll out the new ISMS you will need to find ways to communicate with the relevant departments and the subject matter experts in your organization. As with ISO 27001 also TISAX expects **top management to commit** to the ISMS and the accompanied way of handling information. Commitment not only includes **providing resources such as budget and people** but also to <u>participate in the mandatory management reviews</u>.

4.2.2 Identifying needed tools and technologies

An ISMS needs to be actively used in order to be effective. A collection of documents being forgotten on your file server will not help satisfy the security needs of the automotive industry.

Identify the most needed tools and technologies to improve the security level. This can include a new firewall (e.g. Firewall as a Service – FaaS), a "Security Information and Event Management" (SIEM) tool or "Mobile Device Management" platform (MDM) or "Intrusion Detection and Prevention System" (IDPS).

As you select the tools, you will need to make sure, they actually satisfy the requirements of TISAX and that of your business. The reporting and monitoring requirements are not available for all solutions on the market.

As some staff will need specialized training, non-critical staff should be provided easy to understand awareness trainings. Picking the right training platform and courseware can take quite some time.

Tools, platforms and training are part of an effective security management. This is how to achieve your information security goals.

5 Implementing TISAX in an automotive company

After knowing what has to be done and having assembled your project team, you will need to transition from preparation to implementation. There are many policies and procedures to be written.

The 4 phases of implementation:

- Develop and implement your policies and procedures
- Implement technical controls
- Implement organizational measures
- Ensure monitoring and continuous improvement

5.1 Develop and implement your policies and procedures

Establish the needed policies and procedures. Make sure they meet the standard's requirements. You will end up with a variety of security policies (e.g., incident response policies). While selecting and writing those policies make them **relevant, practical and effective** for your organization. Get support from your stakeholders by involving them in the draft and final version of each document group.

After writing the policies, you need to get them to become part of business life. Establish them and include methods to **enforce** them. Consider ways not only to implement but also to **monitor** them.

As an ISMS is used, you will need to **regularly review** the documentation, **update the content** and make every affected person aware of the implemented changes. Over the years, TISAX has been updated and gained new or refined requirements. In order to remain compliant, one needs to **update the ISMS** to reflect the current standard and address issues known in the current security environment.

5.2 Implement technical controls

Technical controls are an important part of implementation. The protection of information needs a **human and technical response** to threat scenarios. Hence, technology must be configured adequately to reflect the desired **settings**. In order to make sure that your controls and settings are adequate, you will need to **test** them.

The best approach is to run vulnerability assessments and penetration tests. This helps to record all weaknesses and fix them before they become a severe problem to the organization. As previously mentioned, controls have to be regularly evaluated and updated. There are a variety of tools and services to help you benchmark your security infrastructure. Make use of **automation** where possible. **Simplify** your monitoring and reporting on the state of your TISAX compliance.

Besides using tools, you need also to have people trained. Otherwise they are unable to properly set and use those tools defending your environment. Develop your training plan to reflect the mandatory tools for effective security implementation. As highly skilled staff is a **scarce resource** in today's world, companies need to **identify individuals** they can further develop to become new experts in important areas of the organization.

Therefore, effective technical controls need to be in place, so to be compliant with TISAX.

5.3   Implement organizational measures

The 3rd part of implementation is to establish organizational measures. These enable the organization to help protect information systems.

Organizational measures should include:

- security awareness and training programs

- incident response procedures

- develop a risk management framework

Every employee must be aware of their **security responsibilities**. The common understanding, that the organization is taking all necessary precautions to be ready for the event of a security incident, is important for the organizational mindset.

The standards like ISO 27001 and TISAX expect you to have a **training plan** in place. In order to be more effective, you need to have several plans according to the different areas of your business.

Hence, the IT department needs much more technical training so to properly manage all the security technology, which is at their disposal. In contrast, an accountant or marketing manager is not going to configure the SIEM.

They need to have a **proper understanding of the threats** and how to make a security minded approach in their daily work. There are so many simple steps a non-technical user can take when receiving a potentially dangerous email.

Hence, non-technical staff needs their **customized security awareness program**. A marketing person is going to be many more hours connected with the internet than an accountant busy recording financial transactions inside the organization. This is why even administrative roles have **different risk exposures**.

We live today in a very connected world, so that even a foreman at the production line has access to emails, since he needs to effectively communicate with HR and Quality Control. This exposes even workplaces in factories to cyber threats. There is no one solution that fits all organizational roles.

If an incident does happen, we will need to make sure it is handled appropriately. Our **incident response procedures** need to be part of documentation. This information must be common knowledge and not hidden in a locker under trash.

Like with fire drills, you will need to conduct regular security exercises. There are a variety of tools from different vendors (e.g. Hornet Security in Germany) which help **test the resilience** of your staff. This way, people actually experience a simulated attack without being warned ahead. This way they behave like they would during a real attack. Afterwards you can explain to people what happened and how in future avoid being fooled by real attackers.

As last part of this section we need to take a look at our risk management, because it is an important component according to TISAX. Your **risk management framework** must be equipped to **identify, assess and remediate risks**. The objective of risk management should be to preserve the required confidentiality, integrity and availability of information as well as the information systems storing that data.

To ensure this objective is actually sustainable, one needs to conduct **regular risk assessments and update risk response plans**. The security tests help validate the capability of the organization to deal with the threats in a satisfying manner.

5.4 Ensure monitoring and continuous improvement

Having an ISMS in place is a great achievement, nevertheless, it needs to be active and in good health. To ensure its <u>effectiveness and relevance</u> to the organization's risk environment, you need to do following:

- Review and evaluate the effectiveness of policies, procedures and controls

- Make adaptations to address any identified weakness or vulnerability

In order to ensure alignment with TISAX standard you should establish review cycles with these actions:

- annual security assessments

- periodic security audits

The sustainability of your ISMS and successful regular external compliance audits are dependent on **your efforts to monitor and improve your ISMS** <u>regularly</u>. Otherwise you will most likely experience a non-compliance with TISAX with a few months or years. People start forgetting and **no longer care** about your policies, procedures and controls.

By <u>integrating monitoring and improvement</u> into your **routine security practices** you will have less effort to remain compliant as well as safe. <u>Plan regular meetings</u> in your *group calendar* so that you can review the current situation. The assessments need not only to be **reviewed** but should be **documented**. Keep in mind that people forget what was agreed on and that sometimes regular attendants might be absent to a meeting with very significant revelations.

Key topics for your review meetings:

- Effectiveness of security policies, procedures and controls

- Identified areas for improvement

- Trends in the threat environment

- Agreements on next measures to address threats (who, due date, resources needed, dependencies)

This way you can adapt your technical controls much faster to address the developments in the threat environment. You will realize, that your organization eventually becomes ahead of the pack. Instead of your organization being **disrupted and damaged** like the rest of the sector, you will have remained mostly unharmed.

Key benefits:

- Well prepared for potential incidents

- Competitive advantages due to output / operative stability

- Proactively responding to new risks

- Ability to assess impact of new vulnerabilities before they are used against the organization

- Updating technical controls and implementing controls with less strain

- ISMS is therefore always up to date and capable of providing an effective defence against dynamic threats

As you gain insights on ideal ways of **handling unforeseen events**, you will be able to adapt your **security awareness programs**. This way, you develop best practice guides matching your organization's characteristics.

6 Getting ready for TISAX assessment

As you have succeeded in developing and implementing your ISMS in accordance with TISAX, you will soon want to get the TISAX assessment done.

You need to understand the scope of the upcoming assessment. Prepare accordingly for the assessment process and identify items that need special consideration. Look out for the issues many other companies run into.

If you are still unsure where you are, then ask for outside help.

6.1 Understand the TISAX assessment scope

An auditor will evaluate your information security management system against the requirements of TISAX. The assessment will cover areas such as:

- Technical security measures

- Organizational security measures

- Policies and procedures

- Training programs

By knowing and understanding the assessment's scope, you will be able to get all documents, systems but also every potentially involved person ready for the auditor's visit.

Dedicate enough time to review your documentation. Does it satisfy all TISAX requirements? Have you researched inside special interest groups, if there are insights into what auditors are particularly checking this year? Each year accreditors tell certification bodies to pay attention to areas, they have found to be a weakness of previous audits (conducted by all the certification bodies they have accredited).

Auditors will look at your risk management and all associated records. There are no companies in the world, where there are no kind of incidents. Everywhere a digital device breaks, gets stolen or lost. The larger the organization the higher the potential chance there has been such an incident. People delete files by mistake, people click on spam links and get infected or hard drives get dropped. Anything can happen within a year.

Make use of the scope to spot weaknesses you might have overlooked. Get someone to look at the documents, <u>who has not been involved with your ISMS project</u>. Ask them for feedback and any random ideas coming to their mind. As silly or irrelevant they might seem at first, maybe the y help you get relevant ideas.

The assessment methodology involves a combination of document review, interviews with key stake holders and onsite sampling as well as testing some of your security controls.

6.2 Prepare for the assessment

While you are getting ready to submit your documentation and to receive the audit ream on site, you will need to complete some important items on your checklist:

- Collect all ISMS related documents
- Collect evidence to support effectiveness of ISMS
- Assemble your TISAX assessment team

The TISAX assessment team will usually be similar to your TISAX project team. You need to expect auditors to call upon such people as they are able to provide insights and evidence about your organizations way of handling security topics.

Make sure to allocate sufficient resources for the entire TISAX assessment process. Have **sufficient staff** for the assessment. Allocate sufficient budget for the expenses related to this certification project (e.g., travel cost, audit fees, software licencing, equipment, external advice).

In order to add **an extra layer of preparation**, you should get external security experts to identify weaknesses in the organizations defence. **Make the improvements** before submitting your documents to the certification body.

Your organization must understand the requirements of the standard. It is not a good idea to focus on paper and technology but to submit the certification request without having conducted the awareness trainings.

Do not let people in the organization ignore the upcoming assessment. Ensure everyone understands **why it is so critical for the company** to become TISAX compliant and successfully pass the audit.

Update your project plan to reflect where you are and what steps still need to be completed. Don't key aspects slip away into the dark.

Make sure following 4 key aspects are in line with the standards requirements:

- Evidence of compliance
- Technical Security Measures
- Organizational Measures
- Readiness Assessment

Auditors will look for evidence of compliance. If they have the feeling that evidence is fabricated or is barely existing, they might consider this to be an non-operational ISMS.

This is what they will look at in regards to evidence of compliance:
- security policies, procedures, controls
- evidence of measures

Technical Security Measures (a.k.a. TOM) will also be part of the assessment. You need to have technical security measures implemented so that staff know what is expected. Otherwise systems (IDPS, SIEM, Firewalls, Routers, Switches, Virtual Machines, etc.) will not be **properly configured**, so that even a non-technical person will <u>quickly spot discrepancies</u> (e.g. admin password being "password").

During the evaluation of existing Organizational Measures, auditors will want to find out, <u>how well employees have been made aware of threats and expected behaviour</u>. If the **staff you trained**, left your company months before the audit, then it is a bit of an inconvenience having to explain yourself: you **didn't hire** new qualified staff and didn't make an effort to **training remaining staff**?

You need to at least fill the gap temporarily by <u>spreading the responsibilities</u> across the existing team/department, until a new qualified candidate has been hired. Even <u>hiring a freelancer</u> for the time being, is better than failing the costly assessment and loosing contracts with major clients.

Finally, your Readiness Assessment will show the level or readiness your organization is in regards to the TISAX standard. Resolve any vulnerabilities in time. Conduct penetration tests to further identify and eradicate weaknesses in your information security.

6.3 Typical challenges and pitfalls

You may encounter some of the following challenges:
- Lack of documentation
- Inadequate security measures
- Inadequate preparation

Let me address each of the 3 mentioned types of challenges:

A lack of documentation will cause auditors to **suspect inconsistency** and **lack of commitment**. This problem arises when either security measures have rudimentary description and guiding content in the core document or when the expected records are not available. It is understandable that not every technical system provides usable and exportable records. Nevertheless, you can still **create your own record manually** and add screenshots (from firewall statistical graphics) into your word document. Inadequate security measures are related to **missing or inconsistent** configuration of systems. Many kinds of software (e.g., CRM, Backup, …) that provide access via user accounts usually offer an **assignable set of roles and permissions**. Check that every key item is properly implemented and configured.

Assessors will sense whether a person is insecure due to this being their first audit or whether they fear an inadequate preparation might lead the auditor to a **severe non-compliance discovery**. It is normal for every person who has never been at the receiving end of an assessment, to be nervous and trying to have everything overly prepared. Hence, make an extra effort to invest time into reviewing all your items and having conversations with all the people, who might be involved during the assessor's visit. This will help you avoid an inadequate preparation and boost your emotional confidence.

7 How the TISAX Audit will be conducted

In this chapter we will be taking a closer look at how to navigate the TISAX Assessment.

- Understanding the assessment process
- Understanding the role of the auditor
- Key aspects during assessment
- Typical challenges and pitfalls

As with any kind of audit according to standards (e.g. ISO 27001:2022) an audit process will consist of several steps (preparation, ..., writing final report).

The auditor will ask several questions, which you are supposed to be able to answer. No one expects you to know the answer to everything. Knowing <u>who to call upon</u> for help in answering a certain question, is always a **great way to include other people** in the assessment.

7.1 Understanding the assessment process

An assessor will assess the policies, procedures and controls of an organization. Having to check a lot of documents and conducts interviews is **time consuming** for everyone. Assessors have a limited time to get everything done. By you understanding the assessment process, you will reach your goals with **less haste and less stress**.

The assessment phase consists of a set of objectives and outcomes. The assessor needs to **thoroughly check** the organization's information security management system. Keep in mind that it is expected and mandatory that the organization conducts a **self-assessment**, by which the organization proves it can identify any gaps or areas for improvements between external assessments.

The external assessment will usually start with a **documentation-based plausibility check** (Assessment level 2; In ISO 27001: Stage I of the audit). The **comprehensive on-site audit** (assessment level 3; In ISO 27001: Stage II of the audit) will look at documentation referenced by the ISMS. This is also where **interviews** help the auditor evaluate, if the staff actually know, how to handle security in the expected manner.

Once the assessor has completed his investigation, the assessment report will have to be **written and uploaded** to the TISAX Platform. An assessment report will consist of findings and recommendations. The organization needs to use these insights to improve its security. Ignoring these issues and not fixing them could cause severe issues at the next surveillance audit.

Once the assessment report has been accepted, the TISAX label will be issued to the organization. This is seen as a **3rd party validation**. The seal can be seen by OEMs and other companies. This published information serves as a verified overview of the current state of the organization's security environment.

7.2 Understanding the role of the assessor

Understanding the role of the assessor helps manage the expectations of both sides. Literature often refers to an "assessor" also as an "auditor". This person needs to be trained and certified in the TISAX Standard.

There is a shortage in TISAX and ISO 27001 auditors (a.k.a. assessor) because of the <u>deep knowledge and experience needed</u>. That is why you need to expect a certification body or assessment provider to require plenty of time ahead, as they have limited resources. You might encounter an audit appointment maybe in 6 or even 18 months. Use the time to become more confident with using your ISMS.

The lead auditor usually is assigned an audit client and arranges all scheduling with the client directly. As soon as the key items are clarified, he will have to gather an audit team. Having the required number of co-auditors is not easy. The larger the client the more audit work has to be processed.

Furthermore, the auditor must be objective, impartial and free of any **conflict of interest**. The last requirement further limits the amount of available auditors, because certification bodies are required to avoid sending an auditor to inspect an organization he currently has or recently had dealings with.

Hence, if a person left your organization 3 years ago in order to become an auditor, this person needs to highlight to the certification body that he had previously worked for that company. If he is currently advising his former employer on how to get the documentation ready for TISAX then he is not allowed to audit his former employer.

If it were not so, the audit would be at risk of losing its confidentiality, integrity and independence. During the auditor training skills like **communicating, handling findings and formulating recommendations** are important. Accept the auditors visit as a great opportunity to gain access to this persons extensive knowledge. Auditors can provide guidance in regards to best practice strategies for improvement of your organization.

7.3 Key aspects during assessment

Key aspects during assessment:
- Scope of the assessment
- Methodology of the auditor

By understanding the Scope of the assessment you will know where to pay more attention to, as some systems will not be part of the evaluation. The scope helps the auditor and the organization be more focused while avoiding waste of resources.

The methodology of the auditor ensures that the audit is conducted in a consistent and objective way. This allows the auditor to communicate his **requests, questions, findings and comments** in a productive way. The auditor expects the organization to comply with his information requests within a reasonable time. He has to process a lot of information and documents. So many policies, procedures, controls and records will have to be evaluated within a limited time.

The **less resistance** the organization displays, the **more time** is available, to gain insights from the auditor's extensive experience.

7.4 Typical challenges and pitfalls

Typical challenges and pitfalls can be summarized as following key problems:
- Incomplete or outdated documentation
- Lack of understanding of TISAX requirements
- Inadequate preparation
- Inadequate technical controls
- Lack of continuous improvement

It will be of benefit to you to go through the following insights into, why they cause so many unnecessary problems for organizations wanting to gain the TISAX label.

Incomplete or outdated documentation

When you started working on your ISMS documentation you were collecting lots of information and records. As you gradually develop your implementer writing skills, the amount of data **can easily hide irrelevant, outdated or inconsistent documents**.

Tip: If you invest some time with your key departments, you can find out what has changed. Update the documentation or remove outdated content.

Before the assessment, make sure documents are complete. Accidents can happen. Deleting paragraphs by mistake or forgetting to add content from a merged document can cause inconsistencies. Auditors have the advantage, that they have not been reading your material hundreds of times over the past 12+ months.

Tip: You become blind towards inconsistencies. Get someone else to proofread your material.

Don't forget to check the documents you are referring to in the ISMS. Maybe some system related records have been renamed, removed or lost.

Lack of understanding of TISAX requirements

When starting a TISAX project, you will at first research what is required to gain the TISAX label. Your material grows and you eventually can believe to know all what is necessary.

It is advisable to take a TISAX implementer Training so to be knowledgeable and avoid unpleasant surprises during the external assessment.

In the worst case, the organization will be downrated because it did not meet the requirements of the standard. You need to understand how to translate the requirements into **your own organizational context**. That is why simply buying some template off the internet is the best way to fail or burn a lot of budget on external consultants trying to fix the template's inconsistencies.

Inadequate preparation

Having the right staff and resources sounds so logical. Unfortunately, organizations often forget to inform all the different stakeholders and staff of the data when the audit will take place on-site. Having the required people being unreachable during the audit can cause unforeseen problems.

Also make sure the required people have cleared a large enough window in their schedule in case the auditor has to reschedule his days flow of interviews and document reviews.

Inadequate technical controls

If your technical controls are only on paper but not in the operational reality of people's daily work, then auditors will recognize inconsistencies. Your technical controls need to satisfy the requirements of the TISAX standard. Your company network, your core systems (e.g., Backup servers, SIEM), and applications (e.g., ERP, CRM, …) are properly secured. A dirty server room makes no good impression. Get your desks and office space cleaned, tidy and fix any broken equipment. Broken power wall sockets are a bad taste of, how serious you take work safety.

Lack of continuous improvement

As with any kind of standard related certification, you will soon find out, that you will be regularly audited over the next few years. This process is similar to the ISO 27001:2022 audit cycle. With TISAX you are also expected to continuously update your documentation and work on internal improvements.

If you do not bother to take care of your ISMS over the period of 12 months, **you can't realistically fix your cracks** within a weekend. The surveillance audit will lead the auditor to clearly identify, that you are not improving your organization, documentation and security.

You have to get a process set up that not only monitors your security but also reminds you of your **monthly activities**. You need to keep reviewing your policies, procedures, and controls. An active ISMS will see improvements and changes taking place over the period of 12 months.

7.5   After the TISAX Audit

After the auditor has finally left your company premises, you will surely breathe a sigh of relief. Make a few notes before going home. Your next workday will be to review your learnings and create your own preliminary to do list.

The auditor might have already provided you an overview of the nonconformities and observations. Start developing ideas how to productively **resolve the weaknesses** and <u>utilize the recommendations</u> you received during the audit. You will need to develop corrective actions and find reliable ways to implement these necessary modifications.

Understand your results

Once you have been given a proper detailed summary on your current state of affairs, you will need to take time to **understand the relevance** and the <u>cause</u> **of the issue**. It is necessary, to understand the results of the assessment, as otherwise you will waste energy and budget on an <u>inadequate response</u> to the nonconformities. You might even implement recommendations in the <u>wrong way</u> and thereby even <u>create for yourself new nonconformities</u>.

Where are you the best at?

As you work through the assessment results, you will also realize that you are actually **good at some key areas**. Auditors look for the strong and the weak spots in an organization's security. You might even have implemented procedures in a very good way so that you have developed for <u>your own organization a best practice</u>. Maybe you can use those insights to **develop a standardized best approach** at dealing with your weaknesses.

Area of nonconformities

There might be issues in your implementation of the TISAX standard. The auditor will highlight these weaknesses as non-conformities. Look for recommendations on how to improve those weak spots. Some auditors provide a guidance with step by step description on how to fix these deficiencies.

Be aware that some accreditation and certification bodies do not allow auditors to provide such detailed description of how to fix your weaknesses.

Risk assessment

If you receive a report with a risk assessment, then you can see how well protected you are. For each area you will receive marks or points or coloured grades. Use this to prioritize your activities to resolve all the weaknesses or inconsistencies.

Plan how to fix what is broken

Now that you have understood what is weak, broken or confused, plan how to fix these areas. Simply make a quick list of weaknesses and troublesome areas. Then work of expanding the detailed description of the problem and cause. Then elaborate on how you think you need to fix the item. Get feedback from subject matter experts in your organization and then get everybody to work on fixing the items.

Once the auditor returns, he expects you to have done your homework!

8 How to get the most out of this book

You can access a range of additional material I have created to supplement this book from my website. This material includes Checklists, short questionaries (use it for your own self-assessment), Introductory videos and previously recorded webinars. Some of the content is in English and some in German.

https://meetchrisbartsch.com/supplement-tisax-book

There is an TISAX implementer training course (see econry.de or **econry.com**). Nevertheless, you will need to invest time into learning the details should you want to write the ISMS documentation by yourself.

If you are considering to switch your career to become an auditor, then you can take the TISAX Assessor course (see econry.de or **econry.com**). That is self-paced video on demand training in English.

8.1   How to get help

This book is quite detailed in regards to strategy, tactics, implementation and equipment. You might have realized, that you are not necessarily stuck but need some sort of guidance.

A shortcut helps you save time and energy.

In the past I have advised clients from around the world. I eventually realized, what most business leaders lack in order to succeed in introducing information security based on standards like TISAX or ISO 27001. Some people try to do it all by themselves but eventually procrastinate. Some people do not follow the route.

Most people want to focus on their key activities as their time and HR capacities are limited. They would like to leave all the complex aspects of such ISMS projects to a trusted team.

At present we have a limited number of accounts we handle. Hence, we only take per month 5 new key accounts. If you and your company realize that you need guidance then we should have a conversation.

Please be aware that we have set us a focus on particular industries and business types we see fit for working with us. This set criteria ensures that we do not take on clients we can't guide to success.
It is absolutely critical, that the client is **capable and willing** to actively work on making success a reality.

You can contact our consulting team at: info@acato.de or via Telephone +49 89 54041070

8.2 Autor's Profile

The author of this book grew up in multiple countries with a variety of business and manufacturing environments.

After secondary school in Germany, the author became an industrial business apprentice (Industriekaufmann) with BMW AG (Munich). During that time he got to see many different areas of the automotive business. This included a trainee assignment at Australia's largest BMW Dealership in Sidney, Australia. He assisted the head of the "electric, electronics and air conditioning" department. During this time he was involved in the documentation of the key electronic components in the core knowledge handbook (a.k.a. *"Weißbuch"*) of the then to be produced BMW model (E46).

After studying informatics and participating in Microsoft's Training program, he worked at a former electronics subsidiary of SIEMENS. Then went on to develop software for ecommerce. He also worked as an Business Intelligence consultant for a Microsoft partner and was part of **KPMG**'s Forensic technology investigation unit.

Later on he founded his 3rd company as a GmbH. Providing special forensics and disaster recovery services to a variety of corporations and government bodies. He has been providing his knowledge at several events for a variety of security services (e.g., **BKA** Mobilfunk Fachtagung, 2015), universities (**FH Aachen**) and industry congresses (IHK, Helpdesk Forum, …).

Eventually he become an advising board member (NE) at an investment company in **Amsterdam** (NL), which used his forensic expertise to <u>protect their investments</u> into new fields of technology. Thereby becoming the president of the management board of their core services unit (Accounting, IT, Consulting & Legal) in **Warsaw** (Poland).

During this, he also contributed to developing **cyber security** and **ESG** related education programs for a new business education unit. Thereby developing a <u>new auditor training approach for ISO 27001</u>.

As a result, his German company expanded into empowering SMEs to improve their information security via consulting, education and audit services. Now companies across Europe get help in developing ISMS documentation and cyber security strategies.

He is also a certified **Lead Auditor.** He is also part of audit teams at several certification bodies (**TÜV Nord**, **TÜV Süd,** etc.) in the ISO 27001 and ISO 9001 (IT industry) standard.

Christian has appeared multiple times on national TV in Germany (Pro7, n-TV) and South Africa (GauTV). Radio interviews included shows on BR2 and Deutsche Welle. He was part of 2 episodes of the science programs "Galileo" broadcasted on the European TV Channel Pro7. Furthermore, several articles were published indifferent magazines in Europe and the US.

During a conversation with *Apple co-founder* **Steve Wozniak** his ideas around training and continued education were confirmed by Steve.

You can find out more about the author and what his current focus is on by visiting his website at **meetchrisbartsch.com**

Or via LinkedIn: www.linkedin.com/in/meet-christian-bartsch/

8.3 Bibliography

Following literature assisted me in writing this book and therefore I am adding them here as references:

ENX (2023), "TISAX Participant Handbook", published by ENX on 23.02.2023, accessed 01.06.2023 at https://enx.com/tphen.pdf/

Weber, Stefan (2021), *"Nachhaltigkeit im Blick"*, Creditreform Magazin, Edition 12, published 12/2021 by Creditreform

Reichheld, F. (2006), *"The Ultimate Question – Driving Good Profits and True Growth"*, Harvard Business Review Press, ISBN 978-1-59139-783-0

Wehrenberg, Immo (2022), "INTRODUCING NEW TISAX LABELS FOR CONFIDENTIALITY AND AVAILABILITY", published by ENX on 28.10.2022, accessed 01.10.2023 at https://enx.com/en-US/news/new-tisax-labels-for-availability/

8.4 Other Books by Christian Bartsch

The Sustainable Idea

The world of business is becoming even more complex. ESG is affecting companies business and funding activities.

This book explains how best make use of ESG while not drowning in endless cycles of creating paperwork.

ISBN: 979-8-8330-3548-1

Information Security based on ISO 27001 Strategies

When you want to gain the ISO 27001 certification, you need to build an ISMS that is adapted to your business and satisfies the standard's requirements. This guide saves you and your team a lot of pain.

ISBN: 979-8-8651-4150-1